# Listen to the Lilies

## Inspiration from the Garden

by Marjorie R. Sharples

*Margie Sharples*

Photographs by Tennyson Williams

LTL Publishing
Columbus, Ohio

First edition

Published by LTL Publishing
1545 Austin Drive, Columbus, Ohio 43220

Unless otherwise indicated, all scripture quotations are taken
from The Wesley Bible, New King James Version, 1990.
Used by permission.

Scripture quotations marked (The Message) are taken from
The Message, copyright by Eugene H. Peterson, 1993,
1994, 1995. Used by permission of NavPress Publishing
Group.

Library of Congress cataloging-in-publication data
        Library of Congress Control number: 2002091125
        ISBN: 0-9719470-0-7

Printed in the United States by BookMaster, Inc.
Mansfield, Ohio

This book is dedicated to my husband, Jerry.

$\mathcal{H}$e loved me,
gardened with me,
and grew with me
during the writing of this book.

# *Acknowledgments*

While writing this book I received unending support from many people. Early encouragement and draft reading were given by Joan Slaughter, Marilyn Murray, my sister, Beth Kaback, and my mother, Lucile Ruggles. Later encouragement came from fellow students in a writer's workshop taught by Tom Mullen at Pendle Hill, a Quaker center for study and contemplation. The title, <u>Listen to the Lilies</u>, was formulated there.

When I first started writing these devotions, Tennyson Williams told me about the Pendle Hill Center near Philadelphia. I had always enjoyed Tenny's photographs and we soon decided to collaborate on this devotional book. His pictures and constant support inspired me while I wrote.

Tom Mullen encouraged me throughout three years of writing by sharing his knowledge of the creative writing process. He read and critiqued during the early phases of my writing and did extensive editing toward the end of the process. His critiques were always useful and energizing.

Late in the process of writing, Carol Padgett of Birmingham, Alabama, became my booster. Her motivating words, humor and wisdom, kept me eagerly writing and rewriting.

My husband, Jerry, was with me throughout the entire process. He was my first and last reader. He accompanied me through the highs and the lows of writing and publishing this book. He was always willing to work in the garden with me. He also spent many hours getting the manuscript ready for printing. It was a special delight to work together on this project.

# Forward

These short devotional writings blend the inspiration gained from gardening, reading, and meditating with my perceptions about life. My faith, parenting, elementary school counseling, and living in loving communities have deepened the insights shared in this book.

After retiring from a twenty year career as an elementary school counselor, I started gardening. I have had time to be quiet, hear and see God speaking through the plants and in the silence. This book is a composite of lessons uncovered in the garden. These lessons are ancient with their roots found in the Bible, other sacred writings, and secular poetry. I continually rediscover their significance as I experience life, and their relevance emerges as I ponder while gardening. The scriptures on which these devotions are based are from the Bible because Christianity is the faith in which I was born and nurtured. These truths could be found in other sacred scriptures I'm sure.

The devotions are organized by seasons and are augmented with original poetry, favorite scriptures, and photographs taken by Tennyson Williams. His sacred images add visual inspiration to the written words.

Come, listen to the lilies.

*Be still and know that I am God.*
(Psalm 46:10)

# List of Pictures

Identity of flowers and page number:

*This picture won the Open Media Award from the Ohio Art Council at the 2002 Ohio State Fair

# *Table of Contents*

## *Spring*

## *Summer*

# Contents (continued)

# Spring

*$\mathcal{A}$ garden;*
*The best place to seek God...*
*You can dig for Him there.*
(George Bernard Shaw)

# Welcome to Our Garden

*J*ust inside the gate to our garden is a flat rock which says, "Welcome to our garden." I'm glad the words say "our" garden. God has shared this beauty with my husband, Jerry, and me. Our perennial flower garden, brightened by a few annuals, surrounds our Ohio home. Being a novice gardener, with a growing faith, I am learning much about God as I begin to understand gardening.

Come on in. I'd love to share our garden with you. Experience the color and variety the Lord has shared with us. Take time to look and to smell. Listen to the lilies. They have much to say as do all growing things. Stay as long as you wish. Stroll a while or just sit down and enjoy. Come in. The gate is open.

# *In The Garden*

"I come to the garden alone
while the dew is still on the roses,
and the voice I hear falling on my ear,
the Son of God discloses.

and He walks with me,
and He talks with me,
and He tells me I am his own;
and the joy we share as we tarry there,
none other has ever known." (1)

*C*. Austin Miles wrote "In the Garden" in 1912. He based the hymn on John, chapter 20. He wrote quickly, following the experience of a deep spiritual moment and composed the music the same day. The hymn was made famous by Homer Rodeheaver who led singing for the Billy Sunday campaigns. It remains one of the most popular gospel hymns today. (2)

Why does this hymn mean so much to me? Well, there is a sentimental connection with my family. I sang this hymn as a child, with my parents and grandparents sitting beside me. Grandma called it her favorite hymn. My grandmother loved her garden, had a personal relationship with God, and I'm confident she talked to God while in the garden. We have sung "In The Garden" many times at family reunions, fiftieth wedding anniversaries, and family funerals. Often, while singing, my tears flow.

But I have more than sentimental attachment.  My desire for a deep personal connection with God is captured by the words I sing.  Does this hymn speak to that need in you?

Read again its words.  Read slowly.  Read aloud.  My thoughts are noted, add your own.

I come to the garden alone   *(Me - only me.)*
while the dew is still on the roses,   *(I come very early.)*
and the voice I hear, falling on my ear,
the Son of God discloses.   *(God talks to me there.)*

And he walks with me,   *(Yes, with me.)*
and he talks with me,   *(Yes, with me )*
and he tells me I am his own;   *(Yes, I am!)*
and the joy we share as we tarry there,
none other has ever known.   *(It is our personal shared joy like none other. I feel surrounded by God while in the garden. I lose myself there, feeling safe, comfortable, soaking up the sun. I know God loves me. I know God respects me. I understand God needs and wants me. I grasp these truths especially in the garden.)*

He speaks, and the sound of his voice
is so sweet the birds hush their singing,   *(God's voice is inviting. I am ready to listen. I hear nothing else; only God speaking to me through his creation.)*
and the melody that he gave to me
within my heart is ringing.   *(What is that melody? LOVE. God is love. We are on earth to share that love with everyone. God shares love through us.)*

And he walks with me,  *(Now, as in the past.)*
and he talks with me,  *(Now.)*
and he tells me I am his own;  *(Yes, I am!)*
and the joy we share as we tarry there,
none other has ever known. *(Others have their own experience with God...but this is mine.)*

I'd stay in the garden with him
though the night around me be falling,  *(I don't want this special time to end.)*
but he bids me go;  *(I must go...I have things to do. I can't always be in the garden!)*
thru the voice of woe,
his voice to me is calling.  *("Feed my sick...Teach my little ones...Take care of anyone who is in pain...Tell others about my love.)*

And he walks with me,
and he talks with me,
and he tells me I am His own;
and the joy we share as we tarry there,
none other has ever known.

*Dear God, Thank you for offering quiet garden moments. Help us embrace them. Lead us often to that special joy we can share with You. Show us how to respond to your guidance which surrounds us. Amen.*

# Digging And Weeding

*The voice of one crying in the wilderness:*
*"Prepare the way of the Lord;*
*Make straight in the desert*
*A highway for our God.*
*Every valley shall be exalted*
*And every mountain and hill brought low;*
*The crooked places shall be made straight*
*And the rough places smooth;..."*
(Isaiah 40:3-4)

In early spring we prepare for new growth in the garden. Books enumerate activities which will permit the garden be more prolific. We remove the winter debris that was blown into the yard during the winter storms. The dead leaves are heavy, soggy, moldy. We weed, edge, fertilize, mulch, divide, and if it is dry...water. This is hard work! Is it drudgery? No. I anticipate the beauty of later spring. Visions of tulips and daffodils drift by my eyes. The perfume of new growth delights my nostrils. There is hope and much enjoyment. Cleanup is actually invigorating.

I think also about my readiness for God to work through me. I need to "Prepare the Way of the Lord" in my life. I must make paths straight for him to come. This groundwork is ongoing. It isn't done once and finished. For any growing, preparation is needed.

So how does one smooth the way for the Lord?

1.   Clear away debris...What gets in my way to a clearer relationship with God?  Is it busyness?  Is it old attitudes?  Is it lack of learning, or lack of involvement?  Help me, God, to move beyond the things which block my path to you.  Help me sweep them away.

2.   Weed...Some weeds are beautiful plants but if in the wrong place or taking control of the garden, they need to go.  What weeds in my life need to be pulled out by the roots so they don't spread?  Perfectionism?  Being judgmental?  Impatience?  It is easier to pull out bad habits when they are little, fresh, and new.  Help me identify, God, which weeds in my life I need to control.  Help me pull them out while they are fresh.  Don't let them get a strong hold in my life.

3.   Edge...Cutting new edges around the garden keeps grass out of the flowers.  It prevents clutter.  What is cluttering my life, God?  Is it a lack of focus?  Too many projects?  Help me sharpen the edges of my life so I can let You in.

4.   Fertilize...We use a well balanced fertilizer in the early spring.  It provides nourishment and a boost as plants have a growth spurt.  How can I feed my spiritual growth?  The discipline of daily devotions that takes me below the surface of God's word, and regular worship with others can fertilize my soul.

5.   Mulch...This extra cover deters weeds.  It keeps moisture in the soil and helps regulate the temperature of the ground so plants grow

at a steady rate. Being among people who are attempting to grow in similar ways can provide support and nourishment for my own development. Bible studies or other small groups enrich my life. Help me, God, find ways to nurture growth toward You.

6.     Divide and multiply...The plant that is split will become two or three. When divided and replanted, a plant thrives and continues to grow. What part of my faith do I need to share, Lord? With whom should I share it? When would be a good time? I know when I share my ideas and understandings, they continue to grow. That is how You work.

7.     Water...A good balance of moisture is needed in the garden. Too much moisture clogs the soil. Too little parches the earth so plants can't grow. Keep me aware of my own needs for irrigation. Through reading, listening, meditating, and participating in worship let me bathe myself in Your "good water." A good balance of study, fellowship, and service will keep me from being bogged down.

*Dear Lord, help us watch for ways we can prepare the path for You. Keep us focused on clearing away debris, weeding, edging, fertilizing, dividing and watering. Help our souls and minds be fertile ground so Your spirit prospers within us. Amen.*

# A Flower

For lo, the winter is past,
The rain is over and gone.
The flowers appear on the earth;
The time of singing has come,
And the voice of the turtledove
Is heard in our land.
(Song of Solomon 2:11-12)

*A* flower was growing in the field. I looked at it, smelled, touched, and picked it. The flower spoke to me. It was beautiful, tiny, simple, but also profoundly complex. From a distance the blossom had seemed insignificant. It was purple in color, and many buds were clustered on one stem. Up close, I saw an intricate bloom, just beginning to flourish. Several buds were opening. A few were fully unlocked, but others remained tightly closed.

*It's just like me! I'm just beginning to bloom. A few parts of me are open for others to know. Some parts are locked up tight. Many other segments are just starting to be accessible. I'm beginning to share myself with others more and more.*

Many similar flowers were in that field, in many stages of blooming. These flowers were like the people around me, all in various stages of blossoming. They were standing in a field waiting to be looked at, picked, smelled, touched, and loved.  Do we live in communities waiting to be noticed?

*But we are not flowers who have to wait to be picked.*
*We are humans.*
*We can pick, feel, look, smell, touch, love.*
*We are human!*
*We don't have to wait. We can act!*

Yes, I'm a little like that flower, just opening up.  Just beginning to blossom.  But I am also human, able and wanting to act and express myself.

*I'm alive!*
*I'm human!*
*I am!*

*God, I need you with me in my humanness.  Be with me in my growing. Help me feel Your presence in my life so that even in my me-ness, I am sensitive to You.  Support me as I open up and bloom.  Enable me to bring beauty to others' lives.  Help me blossom as do the flowers in the field.  Amen.*

# The Wonder
# of Watching and Waiting

*Wait on the Lord;*
*Be of good courage and*
*He shall strengthen your heart;*
*Wait, I say, on the Lord!*
*(Psalm 27:14)*

*J*oyce Sackett writes, "The secret of the garden is the wonder of the present moment, to notice and revel in it.  It is to love what one has, however small, to see in each day's gifts the goodness and greatness of our God.  If we are only looking forward to the blossoms or the full leaf or pepper that will one day be on the plant, we will miss the beauty that today has to show us."(3)

Being away opened my eyes.  We had just returned from a week in Tucson.  There we were charmed by desert gardens.  We savored the dry landscape of the Saguaro National Park with its gigantic 200 year old saguaro cacti. Little blossoms waited for rain to coax them out, and birds and other wildlife let us know there was much to live for in this dry place.  At the Tucson Botanical Gardens, we viewed a cactus and succulent garden, but we also enjoyed a butterfly garden, a wildflower garden, and a backyard bird garden.  We learned about xeriscapes, which use little precious water yet provide abounding beauty.

A third day we visited six private gardens in the city. Each was unique. We were amazed by the variety of plant life that thrives in a desert climate. We were awed by the profuse blossoms we found blooming where water had been used. It was early spring and the roses were at their peak along with snapdragons and poppies. Many different wildflowers were abundant. Even the cacti exhibited blossoms.

After immersing ourselves in those gardens, we came home and looked at our garden with fresh eyes. Early spring had also arrived. There was no riot of color but much had changed in the week we were gone.

I can wonder, watch, and wait in our Ohio garden. The Bradford pear trees are fully blossomed. The azaleas have bloomed. Tiny leaves are showing on the red maple, red stemmed dogwood, and along the hedge. The red bud is covered with small pink buds and the crabapple tree, which struggled last summer with a blight, is promising to flourish. Thank you, dear Lord, for this beauty. Thank you for the invitation to look and wait as your world again begins to show growth.

So much beauty waits in the potential of a garden. I have taken time each day this week to look at the garden...to watch...to wonder...to wait. In one day the hostas changed from tiny shoots to three and four inch blades almost ready to unfurl into leaves. The bleeding heart grew new branches each day. The anemone presented a gorgeous blue blossom with a deep black center. The candytuft appeared green one day and full of tiny white buds the next. I noticed the trillium and Virginia bluebells peeking through the ground and the ferns starting to unfurl. It was all a miracle! And while I was watching, the birds serenaded with trills and chirps. Thank you God, for time to wait and wonder.

Earlier in my life I often missed the excitement of the early garden. I was anxious for it to be in full bloom. I only saw the beauty in the vivid color. I didn't recognize the splendor of the growing process. I missed the joy of watching and waiting.

The commentary in the Wesley Bible, (Psalm 25:21) states: "To wait for the Lord is an expression of complete trust...Very often God asks people to wait precisely as an exercise in trust."(4) It is difficult to develop and practice patience. So often I want patience and I want it now! Trusting in God's timing makes life easier. I know the garden is going to bloom. I trust in that fact and that makes waiting easier. Faith allows me to relax and enjoy the beauty of the process. Trust offers the same outcome for everyday living.

What about other parts of my life? When I was pregnant, I was so eager for that new baby to be born. Did I miss some of the wonder of the process? When I am learning something new, I seem to want to know it right now. I don't want to study, practice, and work. Jerry and I are retired. How do we wonder and watch during this time in our lives? If I trust God is with me, I can relax and relish the experience. Knowing God is near me, I can be calm and delight in the beauty of the day, whatever it brings.

*We know, God, You are with us everyday. How can we miss You when we are open, ready, and waiting for You? You grasp our hands and open our ears and eyes. You show us the little green shoots of life and tell us You are there. You make us aware of ways we can relate to others so Your love can be experienced. Assist us in waiting for you, in our gardens and in our lives. Help us trust You in all we do. Amen.*

# Spring Rain

*Sing to the Lord with thanksgiving;*
*Sing praises on the harp to our God,*
*Who covers the heavens with clouds,*
*Who prepares rain for the earth,*
*Who makes grass to grow on the mountains.*
(Psalm 147:7-9)

*T*he rain taps on the window at 6:00 on a dark Sunday morning. We've been living with gloomy days all winter, and today I awaken to rain, a refreshing, cleansing shower. It will soak the garden soil. It will replenish any water shortage. The new plants will gulp it down and send their roots deep to nourish themselves.

God's love is like that, coming when I need it. Refreshing me. Allowing me to send my roots deep for sustenance. Sometimes I don't want to see the rain. I want another sunny day so I can play. But a year of sunny days does not a beautiful garden make, and a life with no struggles is not a piece of cake.

My response to rain is intriguing. This morning I welcome it as a positive event. We need the moisture and I greet it with a lifted spirit. But sometimes showers become downpours, or thunderstorms, and I shrink from them. Storms can ravage a garden. The same can happen in one's life. Turmoil threatens us and we are afraid.

Sometimes we try too hard to keep life struggle-free. We frequently measure our success by material means: our prestigious job, our car(s), our clothes.  As parents we try to protect our children from disappointments, even from challenges. We may rush in to solve their conflicts and they don't learn how to take care of themselves.  They don't develop the strength which comes from facing difficulty.  We don't understand that, like rain, struggles can be positive.

When I look back at my parents' lives, I see some storms.  It rained a depression.  It poured several wars.  It drizzled many moves and job changes.  Through these challenges they grew strong.  They reached deep and they found strength.  Family helped, friends assisted, and their faith grew.

All of us can find growth during challenging times, when we look for strength from our Lord.

*Help us, Lord, be alert to the faith-growing possibilities that come when we face challenges. Open us. Assist our seeing. Deepen our feelings. Heal us. Don't let us run away and hide from the pain that comes. Let us feel refreshed by the rain that has to come to cleanse and nourish us. We know You are with us all the time. Amen.*

# Rabbits, Bugs, or Slugs?

*He who dwells in the secret place of the Most High*
*Shall abide under the shadow of the Almighty.*
*I will say of the Lord, "He is my refuge and my fortress;*
*My God, in Him I will trust."*

*Surely He shall deliver you*
*From the snare of the fowler*
*And from the perilous pestilence.*
*He shall cover you with His feathers,*
*And under His wings you shall take refuge;*
*His truth shall be your shield and buckler.*
*You shall not be afraid of the terror by night,*
*Nor of the arrow that flies by day,*
*Nor of the pestilence that walks in darkness,*
*Nor of the destruction that lays waste at noonday.*
       (Psalm 91:1-6)

*W*e had a problem. Was it rabbits, bugs, or slugs?
The newly planted seedlings looked pathetic. Only little
sticks remained. When we planted them, they were vigorous
and strong. Later all the leaves were nibbled to the core.
There was no new growth. Both the marigolds and the
dahlias were decimated. Their potential was wiped out in
just a few days.

We sprayed them with diluted tabasco sauce. My
sister, Laura, said that would work, but it didn't seem to make
a difference. The rabbits probably wanted the recipe for the

salad dressing. "Hum," I wondered. "Was it rabbits or was it bugs? Maybe it was slugs!" Before I could deal effectively with these pests, I needed to find out who they were. We consulted books, the internet, and talked with neighbors.

Occasionally life is like that. Sometimes I am upset about something and I react quickly. Usually if I'm angry, something else is going on. Perhaps I am over-tired or under stress. If I deal only with the anger, I miss what is really causing the problem.

As a human being I have the opportunity to pray, study, think, and then respond to whatever and whoever my enemies might be. It is more effective to search out and understand what is going on in my life, than just to react quickly to the first impulse. I don't have to deal with the problem alone. The Creator is with me and will help me sort out what I need to do. God has provided me with family, friends, and professionals who can help me confront those issues too tangled for me to conquer by myself. God works to strengthen me while I'm struggling with my personal pests.

*Help us know, God, that problems are for solving and growing through. Let us feel Your presence in the process. Lead us to You when we need direction. Relieve us of our fear of struggle. May our faith grow, and also our ability to live the life You want us to live. Amen.*

*I love spring everywhere,*
*But if I could choose*
*I would always greet it*
*In a garden.*
  *(Ruth Stout)*

# *Cindy's Lesson*

*Though I walk in the midst of trouble,*
*You will revive me;*
*You will stretch out Your hand*
*Against the wrath of my enemies,*
*And Your right hand will save me.*
(Psalm 138:7)

$I$t was early March, 1982. It had been a snowy February. Jerry had been out of the country for over a month on a business trip. I had been extremely busy with my own job, taking care of the family alone, grocery shopping, feeding Rags, our dog, and preparing for company. Friday, late in the afternoon, our daughter, Cindy, came home. She was a college student living in an apartment near campus. The next day her boyfriend, Tim from Arizona, was coming to meet the family for the first time. He was spending his spring vacation with us, and I knew Cindy wanted us to make a good impression on him.

The house was clean, the menus were planned, the shopping was done, but I had not gone outside to clean up a month's supply of Rag's deposits. Jerry usually did that job, and I had overlooked it. Besides, the snow had kept it well hidden, so no one had noticed. But the snow had melted that week and Cindy did notice. She was concerned it would be the first thing Tim would see when he arrived.

She suggested that someone needed to go out and clean up the yard. Since it was her boyfriend who was coming, I reasoned she could do that chore.  After a lengthy discussion, she finally took the necessary equipment outside, and under protest, proceeded to clean up all the piles left by Rags.

She was outside a long time.  It was a sizable job! She worked first in the front yard where Rag's contributions were most noticeable and then moved to the back yard which had a southern exposure. The snow was completely gone and the piles loomed. Later, she knocked excitedly on the back door.  I opened it and she called, "Mom, come out here!"  There, right next to the steps bloomed a small bunch of the most beautiful crocus one could ever see, the first sign of spring.  We'd never before seen crocus this early.  These words flew out of my mouth, "See Cindy, sometimes when life gives you a mess to pick up, you find flowers!"

*Keep us alert Lord, to all the "flowers" blooming in our lives, even when our days may be cluttered with messes.  Help us be open to You in the tensions we face.  Keep us looking for You even while we rush about living our lives.  Interrupt our hurry.  Slow us down.  Guide us to notice and appreciate the beauty all around us. Amen.*

# Psalm 150

(<u>The Message</u>, p. 743)

*H*allelujah!
   Praise God in his holy house of worship,
         praise him under the open skies;
   Praise him for his acts of power,
         praise him for his magnificent greatness;
   Praise with a blast on the trumpet,
         praise by strumming soft strings;
   Praise him with castanets and dance,
         praise him with banjo and flute;
   Praise him with cymbals and a big bass drum,
         praise him with fiddles and mandolin.
   Let every living, breathing creature praise God!
         Hallelujah!

# Grieving in the Garden

*Blessed are those who mourn,*
*For they shall be comforted.*
(Matthew 5:4)

*I*t is May 4th, a gorgeous day! The sun is shining...reflecting off the golden tulips. The birds are singing, but I am sad. How could I be sad on such a day?

The tulips are splendid, but they won't last. More than a hundred and fifty of them strutted in full glory last week. Now only a few blossoms stand tall. Most are gone, only their green leaves are left. I don't want tulip time to be over. I don't want the loveliness to be gone.

I know tulips have a life cycle. Just because the petals fall doesn't mean they are gone. They are very much alive. The process goes on. Leaves will catch the sun, nutrients will be produced, and a new bulb will grow. The leaves will drop and add nourishment to the soil. I will see nothing until next spring when they return. I'll forget about them this summer when some other plants grow in their space. But today I am grieving. I don't want this magnificence to leave me.

My dad left us this year. He too was strong and beautiful. Sometimes I didn't pay much attention to him. I was busy with my life and the growing of my own family. I know I missed much of his beauty. I couldn't take it all in. Now I miss him. I always will. But, like the tulips, he lives on. I cannot see him but I feel his energy. I remember his jokes and stories. I always knew when he was near by the boom of his hearty laugh. The cardinals he carved from walnut occupy a sacred spot in my living room. I treasure a picture of him holding our granddaughter, Christen, when she was only two. I can see the love in his eyes and feel the strength in his arms as he hugged her. I have marvelous memories of the love he shared with all.

*I'm grieving in my garden, Great Comforter, but I feel You here with me. Thank you for the tulips. Thank you for my dad. I am grateful for Your love which Dad shared with me. I value my life which he gave to me. Thank you also for this sorrow which is part of life on earth. It lets me know how much I love and feel and miss. Help me share this love, Your love, with others as Dad shared it with so many. Amen.*

# Jack's Back!

*J*ack's back!
What do you think of that?

Jack's Back??
I thought he wasn't coming.

JACK'S BACK!
What DO you think of that?

JACK'S BACK!!
He even brought two more with him.

JACK'S BACK!!!


This silly little poem came to me yesterday, May 4th. Jerry and I had been watching and waiting for the jack-in-the-pulpit, but he hadn't shown his head this spring. We saw some others blooming last week in a wildlife preserve, so we thought we had lost our Jack over the winter. We were saddened by that idea. What excitement we experienced when Jerry found him. He was hiding under some leaves. He had been there all the time and we had just overlooked him. I'm glad we kept hunting. We could have missed him completely had we given up.

Other treasures are surely all around me. I need to search them out. I want to be alert so I don't miss them when they are so close.  I must cultivate my life in order for overlooked riches to appear.  Noticing aromas while cooking, hearing harmonies and rhythms while enjoying music, feeling the emotions of a friend when looking in their eyes are riches indeed.

*Help us, Lord, to define the real treasures in our lives.  May we hunt for them and recognize them when they are just starting to grow so we can feed them and care for them.  May we remember that these gems are gifts from You, and  celebrate and rejoice! Amen.*

# Summer

*Come forth into the light of things,*
*Let nature be your teacher.*
(William Wordsworth)

# Bird Songs

*Be still, and know that I am God;*
*I will be exalted among the nations,*
*I will be exalted in the earth!*
(Psalm 46:10)

Birds are a vital part of our garden. We feed and watch them daily. In the summer they are busy and noisy, demanding our attention. I hear the male cardinal...but where is his mate? I can't see her. There she is. She twitters. She tweets. Her little ones peep. They want to eat.

These bird songs are like God calling me. I wouldn't hear the birds if I was inside with the windows shut. I wouldn't know they were there if I was busy rushing around. But when I sit still, and focus, I notice them everywhere, both close and far away. The beautiful songs are almost drowned out by an airplane taking off. Only if I concentrate, can I hear them. When the plane is gone, the songs again resonate.

Just like God! When I don't focus, I lose God in the roar of the phone calls, demands of my "do list," enticements of today's culture. But the Lord is still there when I open myself up. God is there when I want to hear. God is there when I listen. God is there and speaks to me.

*Thank you God, for being always with us. Keep us alert and focused on You and the beauty of Your world. Help us be still, and know that You are God. Amen.*

*The Amen! Of nature*
*Is always a flower.*
(Oliver Windell Holmes)

# My Grandmother...A Rose

*The wilderness and the wasteland*
*Shall be glad for them,*
*And the desert shall rejoice and blossom as the rose;*
*It shall blossom abundantly and rejoice,*
*Even with joy, and singing.* (Isaiah 35:1-2)

*R*ight now on our fence three ramblers bloom. They
are heavy with blossoms, bringing much loveliness. Some
buds are closed up tight, new, afraid to give themselves.
Some are opening a little and promising great things. Others
are in their prime. They are divine! A few are gone, having
given their all for my joy.

My grandmother, Rose, is gone, having given herself
for all who knew her. I think about her as a bud. She was
tiny I'm sure. She always was. I wonder what she was like
as a small blossom. Was she full of spark and spunk,
struggling to bloom? I've heard of her as a growing flower,
loving her children and their families, giving support and
challenge, giving encouragement, growing food in her
garden, setting goals for her children, growing love in her
home.

I knew her as a full flower, playing cards with me,
baking pies, reading, going to church camp with the youth.
Even though she was a grandmother, she was young. She
shared her time, her thoughts and ideas, her energy, her
hugs.

I remember her as a strong flower, planning for her old age, wanting to be independent. I knew her as an aging bloom, driving back and forth to Florida. Sitting by Grandpa's side when he was ill. Reading a "National Geographic" while he slept...still giving, still loving.

My grandmother, Rose, is gone, having loved a lot. But is she gone? I think not. She lives in me, in the love she gave me which I want to give to others. I pattern my life on hers. She is in my drive, in my ambition to be a loving person, in my desire to grow and give. She is alive in my love of God. She lives in my desire to share.

It is beautiful to think of all the ways a rose can be loved, and given, and known. My grandmother was a rose and I thank God for her. You are a rose too, and I thank God for you.

*I thank You today Lord, for the many people You have given me in my life. Through these relationships You have given love, acceptance, guidance, and forgiveness. You have worked through persons to touch me. Individuals have been roses in my life. Help me remember that most roses are exquisite but they also have thorns. My thorns assist my growing. Others' thorns invite my forgiveness. Thank you for all who share Your love. Amen.*

These thoughts were written on June 7, 1975 in memory of my grandmother, Rose Sherlock Ruggles, who had just died.

# *God is in The Garden*

*Therefore, my beloved, as you have always
obeyed, not as in my presence only, but now
much more in my absence, work out your own
salvation with fear and trembling; for it is God
who works in you both to will and to do for His
good pleasure.*        (Philippians 2:12-13)

*T*hese verses meant little to me when I first read
them.  Then I looked at the annotations that accompanied
the text;  "Living the Christian life requires our choices and
work - but (is) energized and made possible by God Himself
at work in us." (1)  That spoke to me!

All of my life I have been part of a believing
community.  I remember being enthralled by the stories told
by Miss Berkibile in Sunday School.  She told the stories
energetically, using vivid images.  Was God speaking
through her?  Music has always touched me in special ways.
Does God use composers, musicians, conductors, to
communicate for Him through music?  My family lived
honest, hard working lives.  They were good people who
shared with others and were trustworthy. They were loving
people.  Was that how God taught me about love, trust, and
hard work?

God invites us to participate in His plan for our earth.
We have a choice.  Sometimes I am too busy to notice the
options I have.  Occasionally, I am so full of myself and my

own accomplishments that I forget God's involvement in the achievement. Now and then, I just plain ignore what is going on in my life. When this happens, I should go to my garden.

In the garden, I can see I am needed. God uses me. I plant, dig, water, and weed. I choose what to plant and where to cultivate. If I put a seedling in a place that isn't right, it will not flourish. It will struggle and die.

When I am gardening, I need God's help. I study to understand the needs of different plants and then I do all I can to provide the essentials. I can't create these plants. I wouldn't know where to begin to create a new kind of plant. I'm sure geneticists know but they, too, work with God. Their knowledge of plants helps them work with the Creator. I depend on fertile soil, adequate moisture, the stimulation of the sun, information from others, and sometimes the muscle power of Jerry, for our garden. That is all provided by our Maker.

I can't garden without God, but on the other hand, God needs me too. I believe that is the way our Heavenly Father set up this world. The garden would soon be overrun with weeds if I didn't work to keep them out. When I deadhead (pick off dead blossoms) the flowers keep blooming. In this world God needs me and you. The Lord works and teaches through us. God loves through us. The Almighty uses us to make this world a better place but we are given the choice to participate. When we choose to do His work and listen to His guidance we assist in God's creation and "It is good."

*Dear God, Thank you for helping us see, in the garden, how much we need You and how You can use us. Keep us always aware of Your creation and our place in it. Use us always. Amen*

*The kiss of sun for pardon.*
*The song of the birds for mirth.*
*One is nearer God's Heart in a garden*
*Than anywhere else on earth.*
(Dorothy Gurney)

# Diversity

*There are diversities of gifts, but the same Spirit. There are differences of ministries, but the same Lord. And there are diversities of activities, but it is the same God who works all in all. But the manifestation of the Spirit is given to each one for the profit of all:...But one and the same Spirit works all these things, distributing to each one individually as He wills.*
(1 Corinthians 12:4-7, 11)

*I*sat on the front porch enjoying the garden. It was full of vines, flowers, and ferns. The variety was beautiful and the contrasts caught my attention. The robin on the fence brought interest and variation. He belonged in the garden as did the ants, bees, worms, and bugs.

Dark green holly, purple and grey Japanese ferns, white blossoms on the sweet spire, white Nancy with green leaves and white flowers were all present. Green hostas with white edges and an evergreen with new light green candles contrasted with the deep red of coral bells. Bees were busy in all of it.

Peeking over the fence was the tall, round, dark purple allium. No other plant was like it. The zebra grass was just starting to grow, displaying light green spikes. The young sedum was a shade of lime. In the back of the garden tall dark evergreens and the white leaves on red stemmed dogwoods stood out. Some plants were low and creeping, some tall and spiky. Many had splendid flowers, both tiny and large. How much more interesting and beautiful was this mix than a garden all filled with one kind of plant. This sight reminded me of the diversity in God's world.

Why is it that different plants live together better than people of various cultures, religions, or races? Do they know something we don't know? Is it that they have learned to live within the Creator's control instead of struggling for their own power?

God has put people of many different cultures on one sphere. We speak many languages. We live in many different ways. We are all God's. We live together and need to learn to respect each other and love each other. Just think of the diverse beauty we could experience if we lived together in acceptance, love, and peace.

*Creator, for the diversity in this world, we are grateful. Keep us noticing, cultivating, and respecting it. Help us learn to live with others in dynamic mixes, honoring the beauty in the variation. Empower us to find and cherish our common traits rather than fearing and hating our differences. Amen.*

# Garden Stakes

*Train up a child in the way he should go,*
*And when he is old he will not depart from it.*
(Proverbs 22:6)

$I$look at our garden the way I look at my family. We have a flower garden full of various perennials, annuals, shade plants, and sun lovers. Aren't families like that too...full of variety?

It takes many components to have a beautiful, bountiful garden: time, nourishment, plants, seeds, interest, tools, energy, patience, good planning, some weeding, and stakes. Aren't these also needed for strong loving families?

I am part of a marvelous family. This family didn't just happen. God has been with us through many generations and experiences. Some were fantastic, many routine, and a few tragic. Through those events God has given us strength.

In the garden we use stakes to make plants sturdier. Some of our plants grow so tall that they droop to the ground. If we put a few stakes around them and use some string, the plants are held up straight and their beauty is clear for all to see. They are stronger and resist the wind and rain.

Some of our plants need a trellis to guide them as they grow. The fall blooming clematis in our garden was planted in front of an old trellis from my parents' home. The clematis was tiny when we planted it, yet grew over eight feet in one summer.  It climbed all over the trellis and when it bloomed the blossoms were up against the house, tall and beautiful; not lying low on the ground, hidden by other vegetation.

Families can be like stakes and trellises.  My family shared its values so we were stronger people.  Those values were our stakes.  They pointed us in the directions we needed to grow.  They held us up when we needed holding.

Think for a moment about some values passed on to you by your family.  Write them down and thank God for those stakes.

Think also about how your family members have been stakes for each other when someone needed support.  Write these down and again thank God.

Think about how you can be a trellis for someone else in your life; perhaps a family member, maybe a friend.  Plan how you will be a stake for someone today and thank God for this opportunity.

A word of caution:  Not all plants need stakes or trellises.  Some need freedom to spread as God wanted them to spread.  People within our families are also like that.  All need care and understanding. If their growing habits show the need for stakes or trellises, have them available and use with love and care.

*Dear nurturing God, I am thankful for the stakes and trellises in my life.  I am thankful for the direction offered, for the support given.  Help me now be aware of ways I can be a stake or trellis for those around me.  Use me to share Your love with those I am near. Amen.*

# So, What is a Weed?

*Then He taught them many things by parables, and said to them in His teaching: "Listen! Behold, a sower went out to sow. And some seed fell among thorns; and the thorns grew up and choked it, and it yielded no crop."* (Mark 4:2-3, 7)

*I*t is summer and time to attack weeds. They are peeking up between other plants. They make the garden look untidy. They are threatening to over-grow the lilies we transplanted by the garage. They must be controlled.

But what is a weed? Eleanor Perenyi says, "If we could bring ourselves to see weeds like this, (beautiful and beneficial) we might be in less of a rush to get rid of them; and organic theory does in fact hold that they constitute a mini-ecology that should be respected. They put nutrients into the soil as well as taking them out, preserve tilth, and some are useful in insect control." (2) She goes on to name many wildflowers which are considered glorious flowers in one setting and weeds in another. When I look at my own garden I see flowers I have purposefully planted which may be considered weeds: Queen Ann's lace, loosestrife, bluebells, yarrow. Ralph Waldo Emerson called a weed "A plant whose virtues have not yet been discovered." (3)

Even though some weeds are beautiful and useful, they need to be kept in control. While on a trip in the south we visited a gorgeous garden called Rosedown, located in

Louisiana. It had been developed and nurtured by a plantation family over several generations. In the early 1900's the garden became a burden to the survivors who lived on the plantation. The three elderly women had little money and more than they could handle caring for the house, let alone tending a garden. The extravagant garden became overgrown. When it was rediscovered in the spring of 1956 it was "choked with jungle-like growth." (4) The ancient camellias and huge azaleas were covered with the growth of weeds gone untouched for years. "One might say that the gardens had run wild, after the experienced, knowledgeable control of Martha Turnbull (the original owner) was no longer there." (5)

The weeds in our garden remind me of flaws in my life. Some beautiful things need to be kept under control so as to not take over. One of these is self confidence. Unbridled it develops into arrogance and haughtiness. It grows into pride. It becomes judgmental in its dealings with others. Another is intelligence. This can put off others when it is flaunted and abused. Poor habits are also invasive weeds. They are extremely difficult to remove.

What weeds in your life require control? How do you go about pulling out these pests? We are never free of them. They demand daily awareness and effort. They require daily prayer.

As in a garden, I can do preventive maintenance. Mulch helps keep many weeds under control. I carefully choose what I plant and where I plant it. If I select an invasive plant, I watch it carefully and remove it from areas where I do not want it. One of the invasive pests in my life is a poor eating habit. I need to be constantly on the alert to what I eat and how it is prepared. Bad habits are hard to overcome. Do you have an invasive habit which controls your life?

We become so dependent on habits to which we cling. A big weed growing by the roses cannot be pulled out with a little tug.  It needs drastic action.  It requires the work of a hoe.   What in your life asks for this kind of effort?

I think I can accomplish most anything.  At times this self assurance is like a blossom opening unfettered to the sun.   At other times it is more like a weed waving in the wind. I have been a successful person.  With achievement comes the confidence that I am the doer.  I am the maker.  I am the one in charge.  This is surely not so.  There is a Creator, who made me in His image, and who must remain the one in control.  I must go to my knees, just as when weeding in the garden.  I want to confess my dependence on God and ask for help in the weeding activity in my life.

*Bring us to our knees, God.  Help us weed out the things in our lives which separate us from You and from others.  Give us awareness.  Provide us with strength to pull out the weeds in our lives.  Grant us the tools to dig deep and get to the root of the evil which tries Your patience and limits us.  Dear God, keep us at this mission daily, so we are in communication with You always. May we become the beautiful creations You intended.  Amen.*

# Listen to the Lilies

*"Therefore I say to you, do not worry about your life, what you will eat or what you will drink; nor about your body, what you will put on. Is not life more than food and the body more than clothing? So, why do you worry about clothing? Consider the lilies of the field, how they grow: they neither toil nor spin; and yet I say to you that even Solomon in all his glory was not arrayed like one of these."*
(Matthew 6:25-28)

*"Give your entire attention to what God is doing right now, and don't get worked up about what may or may not happen tomorrow. God will help you deal with whatever hard things come up when the time comes."*
(Matthew 6: 34, <u>The Message</u>, p. 24)

$\mathcal{L}$ilies...there are so many kinds, so many colors; golden, mauve, red, salmon. They add splendor to our garden all summer and into the autumn. There are oriental lilies, Asiatic lilies, daylilies, stargazers, Easter, and even the common old privy lilies.

In the last few years we have been introduced to daylilies by the gift of root stock from friends. We planted them in various parts of our garden, not knowing much about them. The first year they were small plants with a few blossoms. The second year they were fabulous. They bloomed at various times, were an assortment of colors, and some added a beautiful fragrance to the air. If I picked (deadheaded) the spent blossoms, some of them continued to bloom for most of the summer.

Matthew 6:28 says, "Consider the lilies of the field, how they grow..." When I "consider" the lilies or "listen" to them, I hear an important lesson about living in the present. An individual blossom on a daylily lasts one day. If I am to enjoy it, I must look at it carefully, pay attention to its special beauty, smell it, and be thankful for its part in my life. If I am in a hurry and don't look, that blossom will be gone tomorrow and I will have missed it. I must focus if I want to receive the gift offered by that lily. I have to slow down in order to "listen" to the lilies.

This is an important lesson. In order to get the maximum from what is offered me each day, I need to concentrate. Good listening involves focus. How many of us have learned to do several things at the same time, scattering our attention? We think we are being efficient. I contend we are diluting our experience.

My children are adults now. Several years ago I was searching for pictures of our son, Steve, when he was young. I wanted to include them in a scrapbook being prepared for his wedding. I found many photos of things he had made: cars, halloween costumes, pictures, lego creations. He spent hours creating. During this time in his life I was going to school and working part-time. I focused on my own agenda more than his. When I looked at those snapshots I was astounded. I didn't remember many of them and yet they were so expressive of his personality and originality. Because I was centered on another part of my life, I had missed some significant moments with him.

*Slow us down, Lord. Help us focus on the commonplace in our lives. Empower us to recognize the blossoms that won't be there tomorrow. Enable us to identify those persons, experiences, and opportunities which are everyday gifts to us from You. Help us "listen" to the lilies. Amen.*

# Summer Means Change

*Daniel answered and said:*
*"Blessed be the name of God forever and ever,*
*For wisdom and might are His.*
*And He changes the times and the seasons;..."*
  (Daniel 2:20-21)

Our garden has helped me see the continuity of life. Each year the plants return. The peonies are bigger this year than last but they are still red, pink, and white. The lilies grow in the same place where we planted them four years ago. The ferns multiplied but we lost the allium. The rambling roses responded to trimming and training so they are more vigorous.

The garden is always in transition and so are we. Our lives grow and change but there is still continuity. There is growth. There is progress and God, the creator, abides with us.

Each time I made transitions in my life I grew. Some of the changes were relatively easy and some were tough. I can still remember the tug when our oldest child, Marilynn started kindergarten. There was uncertainty. Is she ready? Will she be safe? Will she succeed? She did, and I found others loved, challenged, and led her. Through the struggle to release Marilynn, I also gained confidence in her capabilities. God was with us during this period of growth.

Then there was birthday # 30. I was no longer a "young" mother. My baby, Steve, was three and there would be no more babies. I was OLD! But I had time to go back to school and learn counseling skills, and God continued to be with me.

The move to Washington D.C., away from the home where Jerry and I had raised our family, presented a challenge. Our children were on their own, and I was away from the secure place where I had lived for seventeen years. I no longer had my reliable job but I found new community and I thrived. During loneliness, I discovered God was with me. I discovered a school in which to work. I made new friends, accepted fresh challenges.

Now there is retirement and the death of parents. There has been another move and another community. What will come next? A chance to "be" instead of "do"? The gift of time to develop deeper relationships? I am still growing and God is with me.

*Lord, thank you for transitions, and the stretching they demand of us. We appreciate the opportunities to grow which they present. Help us be always aware of Your nearness, Your stableness, Your steadfastness, which brings security and flowering in the midst of change. Amen.*

# Around, Around, Around We Go

Around, around, around we go
  From birth to death we flow,
  From ground so bare to waves of bloom,
  Around, around we go.

Around, around, around we go
  From child to teen we grow,
  From early bulbs to deep deep snow,
  Around, around we go.

     And God, the creator is with us in all.
     God, the starter, the protector, the energizer...
      God is with us in all.

Around, around, around we go
  From young with plans so grand,
  To older ones with duties to face,
  Around, around we go.

     And we must live,
     And we will work,
     And we can love,
     And we may weep.

And we will grow,
And we may go,
And we can give,
And we will get.

And God, the creator is with us in all.
God, the starter, the protector, the energizer...
God is with us in all.

Around, around, around we go.
In and out and to and fro

From doubt to strength,
From safety to danger,
From success to defeat,
From disappointment to challenge.

Around and around we go.

And God the creator is with us in all.
God the starter, the protector, the energizer...
God is with us in all.

# Connecting

*And He said, "The kingdom of God is as if a man should scatter seed on the ground, and should sleep by night and rise by day, and the seed should sprout and grow, he himself does not know how. For the earth yields crops by itself; first the blade, then the head, after that the full grain in the head. But when the grain ripens, immediately he puts in the sickle, because the harvest has come."*
(Mark 4:26-29)

*O*ur garden encourages connecting. While I work in it, people stop and comment on what is growing or ask me a question. We chat awhile and become better acquainted. Were the garden not there, they would walk right by, with at most, a smile or short greeting. My neighbor brought over some plants she wanted to thin out. They add nicely to what I have. The White Nancy in our garden is spreading and will soon take over the world, but we are finding many who would like to have some in their gardens. "Come and help yourself," I say.

The garden has also helped me build bridges over the generations. Both of my grandmothers were gardeners. Jerry's mother, Bernice, always had flowers to give away. She grew an entire area of white flowers, planted at various times to ensure she would have altar flowers for her small country church. I was genuinely touched a year ago while attending the same church.  On the altar were flowers grown, arranged and delivered by her granddaughter, Mary Lou.  How significant it was that Mary Lou had also been inspired by her grandmother's growing and giving.

Like memories and inspiration, plants can be passed across generations.  Last week I took a large bouquet of red peonies to my ninety year old mother.  These peonies came to me from her mother by way of my sister, Laura.  Grandma Otis had given Laura a start when Laura moved into a new home and Laura provided me with some when we began our present garden.  Now I can divide them and present them to my children.  How special to say, "These peonies came from Great Grandma Otis's garden."

The connection continues.  My grandson, Ben, gave me a packet of Texas bluebonnets to sow in my garden.  I'm not sure they will grow in Ohio but they will have a chance.  My granddaughter, Christen, took cuttings from our garden to try in her own.  We connect meaningfully when we are together enjoying the garden.  I hope someday they will enjoy the beauty of their gardens with their own grandchildren and remember our times together.

As I have given away plants, my garden has grown and so have I.  I have given new starts of plants to my sisters, Ann, Laura, and Beth, and they have given to me.  I have learned names of flowers, their habits, where to plant and where not to plant.  I have been introduced to new perennials and annuals.  I have been stretched and invigorated.

Perhaps the same would happen if I dared to share my faith more with others.  My beliefs have been nourished by my family and passed down through generations.  My faith has grown whenever I had courage to speak of it with others.  Too often, when I have the opportunity to express my faith I keep quiet and think, "Actions speak louder than words."

Here is where I need to take risks and grow. My faith is a gift from God which continually develops. Voicing where I am in my own faith journey helps me stretch, and it may strengthen another person's beliefs. I don't have to have all the answers. I need only communicate where I am, in the same loving manner as I give a flower or offer a gardening idea.

*Enable us Lord, to make connections with others. Help us be willing to share our faith. Enable us to verbalize our beliefs. Fortify our relationships as we continue to communicate with each other about our understanding of You. Amen.*

# Isaiah 58:11

*The Lord will guide you continually,*
*And satisfy your soul in drought,*
*And strengthen your bones;*
*You shall be like a watered garden,*
*And like a spring of water,*
*whose waters do not fail.*

# Jack's Back #2

*J*ack's back!

> He's over two feet tall!
> He's taller than the bird bath...
> > What do you think of that?

> He has his pulpit for all to see.
> He stands so tall...as proud as can be.
> And clustered below the mammoth leaves
> > Are eight tiny, little babes.

JACK'S BACK!!

> What DO you think of that?

*The glory of the garden
lies in more than
meets the eye.*
(Rudyard Kipling)

# Autumn

*Why is it that so many of us persist in thinking that autumn is a sad season? Nature has merely fallen asleep and her dreams must be beautiful if we are to judge by her countenance.*
(Samuel Taylor Coleridge)

# The Cat in the Garden

She moves very slowly.

She moves, one small foot at a time.

> Step...pause...look...listen
> Step....pause....listen....look.....crouch.....
> Step.....be still.....look.....listen
> Step......listen......look......don't move......
> look...smell...stay low...look high...
> listen....look....listen.....look again......
> lay low......stay still......don't move......

Her tail twitches.

It's right there.

Don't move.

Wait.

CHARGE!

Rats!

# *Drought*

*Parched ground that soaks up the rain and then produces an abundance of carrots and corn for its gardener gets God's "Well done!"*
(Hebrews 6:7, <u>The Message</u>, p. 466)

*T*he clematis was pleasing in July. Its blooms dangled on the fence. I should have observed, however, that the blossoms were smaller than usual and fewer in number than last year. In August the bottom leaves turned brown and dropped off, and then I noticed. They needed water. We sprinkled and fertilized before they bloomed but afterwards, we neglected them. They suffered, but I didn't see.

On the far edge of our garden were some marigolds. They must have been just out of the range of the sprinkler. We had to irrigate weekly because it had been a dry summer. These marigolds looked pitiful. They were shriveled and the blossoms dropped off before they opened. A foot away where the ground was moist, their sisters were large and full of big blooms.

The white impatiens told us when they needed soaking. Their leaves curled and the few blossoms drooped. It seemed we needed to drench them all the time. They were next to bushes that stole moisture from them. Near the impatiens were hostas that suffered, too. The hostas did not bloom at all that summer. Their showy leaves lay limp on the ground. I sprinkled them. The ground around them was hard and the water ran off. Jerry showed me how to work up the soil, build a little dam around each plant, and then fill it. The moisture soaked in quickly and I filled each well again, and again. The plants responded. It required noticing, knowledge, and patience...not just a quick run by with the watering wand.

All these plants needed more water than we gave them. The season was very hot and dry. We didn't realize what some needed. We didn't watch closely. We just couldn't give enough to others. We tried but we weren't able to keep everything beautiful.

This makes me think about the needs of people around me. Do I pay enough attention to others? Do I notice when their spiritual well is going dry? It requires intimacy. This level of sharing takes time and effort. I need to be with others in order to understand their concerns. Sometimes that demands more than I want to give. I'm impatient. I want to "water them quickly." But if they aren't ready, or they hurt so much they are closed, what I have to give will not be useful. I have to wait and love. I must listen carefully to hear their needs. I need to build a reservoir of trust with them. I pray that I am working with God in this "watering."

*O Divine Healer, open our eyes, ears, and hearts when we are with others. Help us be aware of their spiritual needs and help us be Your channel. Strengthen us so we can be useful in Your work on this earth. Amen.*

# Spiritual Drought
## (Another look at drought)

As the deer pants for the water brooks,
So pants my soul for You, O God.
My soul thirsts for God, for the living God.
When shall I come and appear before God?
My tears have been my food day and night,
While they continually say to me,
"Where is your God?"   (Psalm 42:1-3)


Spiritual drought, we all have faced it. It is when we close up tight to protect ourselves from the hurts of the world.  In tightening up we push others away, including God. We drive away the very comfort for which we are hungering. We shrug off caring.  We can't hear empathy.  We shove away love.  We close up so tight. God can't get in at the very moments of our greatest need.  We are like the rhododendrons whose leaves curl up to conserve moisture in the middle of a very hot day.

God is always present.  God wants us to be open, even when we are hurting.  God uses other people to care for us, to "water" us, during these times if we will let them.

*Help us, Comforter, open up when we are hurting.  Give us trust enough to  risk.  Even if it is just a little, it is a beginning.  Make us aware of Your love through other people.  Help us know we are not alone. Amen*

# Luke 8:11-15
## The Story of the Seeds

*A*s they went from town to town, a lot of people joined in and traveled along. He addressed them, using this story: "A farmer went out to sow his seed. Some of it fell on the road; it was tramped down and the birds ate it. Other seed fell in the gravel; it sprouted, but withered because it didn't have good roots. Other seed fell in the weeds; the weeds grew with it and strangled it. Other seed fell in rich earth and produced a bumper crop.

"Are you listening to this?
Really listening?"
His disciples asked, "Why did you tell this story?"
He said, "You've been given insight into God's kingdom - you know how it works. There are others who need stories. But even with stories some of them aren't going to get it:
`Their eyes are open but don't see a thing.
Their ears are open but don't hear a thing.'

"This story is about some of those people. The seed is the Word of God. The seeds on the road are those who hear the Word, but no sooner do they hear it than the Devil snatches it from them so they won't believe and be saved.

"The seeds in the gravel are those who hear with enthusiasm but the enthusiasm doesn't go very deep. It's only another fad, and the moment there's trouble it's gone.

*"And the seed that fell in the weeds - well, these are the ones who hear, but then the seed is crowded out and nothing comes of it as they go about their lives worrying about tomorrow, making money, and having fun.*

*"But the seed in the good earth - these are the good hearts who seize the Word and hold on no matter what, sticking with it until there's a harvest.*
(<u>The Message</u>, p.139-140)

*Everything that slows us down
and forces patience, everything
that sets us back into the slow
cycles of nature, is a help.
Gardening is an instrument of grace.*
(May Sarton)

# Seeds of Promise

*Then He said, "What is the kingdom of God like? And to what shall I compare it? It is like a mustard seed, which a man took and put in his garden; and it grew and became a large tree, and the birds of the air nested in its branches."* (Luke 13:18-19)

*A*utumn is a time to notice seeds. They are produced in such abundance. Some are travelers that attach themselves to socks and slacks. Others are sunflowers with heads so heavy, they droop with the weight of seeds. This fall I was fascinated with the seed pods of the cleome in our garden. Each plant had produced myriad pods. I wish I had counted how many were evident on one flower stem. The pods, when they burst open were overflowing. Had I counted the kernels in every pod, I could offer a scientific report.

The cleome flower sits at the top of a stem that can grow to the height of four feet. As the stem grows it carries the blossom with it. The blossom develops many seed pods as it moves up the stem. Think of the potential. It takes just one seed in the right place to produce this prolific plant. Just one! That plant, in turn, produces hundreds, perhaps thousands of seeds. What a marvel.

In order for the garden to flourish and thrive, thousands of seeds are produced. Some of these land on good soil,  some on poor, some on well tended soil, and some are eaten by the birds.  With the great multitude of seeds, there is promise.  God has a plan for the garden.  In order for plants to continue, they must reproduce.

Seeds are meant to be planted.
Seeds are meant to grow.
Seeds are meant to thrive.
Seeds are meant to go.
Without going, there can be no growing.
Without growing, there can be no going.

If I equate myself with being God's garden, I am full of rich and fertile ground.  Many kernels of God's love fall on my soil and germinate.  I believe God has lavished me with all needed for an abundant life.  Weed seeds try to establish themselves but the "Great Gardener" is vigilant and tugs them out.

If I see myself as a thriving plant in God's garden, I know I need to produce seeds.  What kinds will I produce? Will they be seeds of love,  of compassion, of forgiveness? How will I spread these seeds?  God will help me with this sowing.

*You have put us in Your garden, God. You started us from kernels of love. You have nourished us all of our lives. We are still growing. Help us sow the seeds that are developing within us. May we share them so Your world will continue to thrive. Thank You for Your plan of growing and going. Help us all be a part of that plan. Amen.*

# The Berries and the Birds

*Finally, all of you be of one mind, having compassion for one another; love as brothers, be tenderhearted, be courteous; not returning evil for evil or reviling for reviling, but on the contrary blessing, knowing that you were called to this, that you may inherit a blessing.        (1 Peter 3:8-9)*

*I* paid little attention to the hawthorne tree in our tiny courtyard garden. In the spring it was covered with small sweet smelling blossoms for a week or so, but I was enjoying the brilliant tulips and didn't notice.  It was just there. In the summer the green leaves provided shade but more coolness came from the large aged red bud in the background and the  grapevine covering the patio pergola.  I hung the bird feeder on a hawthorne limb so I could observe the feeding birds from my kitchen window.  It was fun to keep track of the action, but I didn't notice the limb holding the feeder. I took the tree for granted.  It was there all the time.  It slowly changed from one season to the next; not demanding notice.

Right now, in late November, this hawthorne is spectacular!  The leaves are gone but it is covered with berries.  The lower wispy branches hang down with the weight.  The light grey bark of the limbs contrasts with the brilliance of the crimson fruit.

The other day, I counted more than a dozen birds flitting through and sitting on its branches. They landed and ate their fill from the abundance. The birds came in several varieties; robins, nuthatches, cardinals, finches. All were feasting at the same time. They ignored the bird feeder. Why bother with seeds when bite-sized fruit was available?

How could I take this tree for granted? Why didn't I sit under its shade and drink in the coolness it offered this summer? Why does it take a knock-out crop of berries for me to realize its worth?

Am I like that with people too? Do only pretty, talented, charismatic, folks attract my attention and interaction? What about the quiet, shy, and less attractive? All are part of God's world. Each has plenty to offer. I could gain much if I took the time to notice, to listen, and to love. I have the opportunity each day to appreciate others, even the "hawthorne people." They won't grab me. They don't shout for my attention. I need to be aware of them and invite them into my life.

*Glorious God, may we experience Your beauty within other persons. Help us take time to get to know their charm at various seasons of their lives. Don't let us take them for granted. Enable us to know You through others. Keep us looking, listening, and loving. Amen.*

*L*ike gardeners,
we need to learn that we can't
plant and reap the same day.
(Anonymous)

# Late Bloomers

*Brethren, do not be children in understanding;*
*however, in malice be babes, but in understanding be*
*mature.* (1 Corinthians 14:20)

The goldenrod is tall and full. We planted it last fall after enjoying it's beauty in the fields and along the roads. Its blossoms are so bright and yellow on the top of long green stems. The autumn breeze blows the stalks back and forth, yet they are strong and will not be blown over. We almost forgot where it was planted. It came up late and was short for a long time. Now, in late autumn, the deep yellow blossoms wave and demand attention. You can't look without noticing the goldenrod.

The mums have also surprised us. We have two large groupings. One is a golden bronze color and the other is purple. They both started from bare little shoots. One was a gift from my sister, Ann, and the other we bought for a quarter at a horticulture sale. The purple ones didn't bloom until after the first frost. We waited and waited for them. Late bloomers can't be rushed.

These lovely delayed blossoms remind me of the necessity and value of trusting and waiting. Some plants are meant to lag in their blooming. They fill the emptiness of the deep autumn with fresh color. Their blooms last long because it is cool. They are on a separate life cycle than other growing things.  Their beauty comes at a different time and they are treasured for their enduring blossoms.

Many people are late bloomers, (LBs).  As LBs grow and mature they gain confidence in themselves.  They find interests and talents they didn't have time for in their younger years.  They take time for meditation and connecting with a higher being in their lives.  They trust inspiration.  They trust themselves.  LBs are willing to take risks.  They are able to cultivate these new talents.

Where are you in your life?  Are you a late bloomer? Could you be one?

What is blooming in this part of your life?
Have you taken time to nurture it?
How can you encourage this blossoming?
Will you share these late "flowers" with others?

*We are often in a hurry in this youth-oriented culture, God.  We look for quick beauty.  The mums and goldenrod remind us of the charm and grace of late bloomers.  May we see in our own lives the value of slow, prolonged, blossoming.  Let us nourish this growth, tend it, treasure it, and eventually share it to Your glory. Help us know its significance.  Be with us in our late blooming. Amen.*

# Putting the Garden to Bed

*For the Lord will not cast off forever.*
*Though He causes grief,*
*Yet He will show compassion*
*According to the multitude of His mercies.*
*For He does not afflict willingly,*
*Nor grieve the children of men.*
(Lamentations 3:31-33)

*A*utumn brings the difficult chore of putting the garden to bed. This entails cutting plants back, dividing, raking and covering plants with leaves. Along with the physical labor I feel a sense of melancholy, a sadness associated with saying goodbye.

I hate saying goodbye! The hugs are long and tears often flow. Over the years there have been many goodbyes for me. Some that come to mind are:

Saying goodbye to my German shepherd, Jan, when we moved to a place too confining for her. I was six and I grieved.

Saying goodbye to my three children as I left them for the first time at the school door.

Saying goodbye to dear neighbors as we moved halfway across the country.

Saying goodbye to a house that had become a place of nurture, while we lived for sixteen years within its walls.

Saying goodbye to our children as they left our home for their own adventures.

Saying the final goodbye to my mom and dad as they took their last breaths.

When I say, "Farewell, so long, Godspeed," part of me goes with those leaving. It must be the tearing away of that part that causes pain. Still I am glad a portion of me goes with them. Our lives are not completely separated. We have shared memories and emotions which bring us comfort in our parting. We have a bond that distance does not erase. Is that link God being active within us?

Several comforting thoughts surfaced as I labored in our fall garden. Saying goodbye, whether to plants or people, is part of the process of life. Life goes on and we persevere. That is what our wonderful existence is all about; growth, change, planting, harvesting, smelling and picking the roses, helping our children grow and watching them go.

Saying goodbye isn't so difficult when we know we'll be together another time. Perennials inform me of that. They will be back next spring. They may be in a new spot, they may be different, but they will be back.

When we say farewell to a loved one it helps to know it is not forever. We can have a new relationship with them. An example is the friendship we are able to develop with our adult children. They are no longer dependent on us and we become companions instead of authority figures. Even in death, a new connection can develop which keeps us close. Goodbye isn't forever.

On my desk is a very small vase with dried lavender. The aroma from it reminds me of our summer garden. Also on the desk are pictures of my grandparents. When I take time to gaze at those pictures, floods of memories come back bringing the love and tenderness I shared with these loved ones. Life goes on. The garden will bloom next spring and summer. Letters and E-mail keep me in touch with family and friends. God is part of me and part of others. That element keeps us close.

Julia Baker's poem says it well. Its name, "Mizpah," comes from a favorite benediction found in Gen 31:47-49. "May the Lord watch between you and me when we are absent one from another."

### Mizpah
by Julia A. Baker

Go thou thy way, and I go mine,
    Apart, yet not afar;
Only a thin veil hangs between
    The pathways where we are.
And "God keep watch 'tween thee and me";
    This is my prayer;
He looks thy way, He looketh mine,
    And keeps us near.

I know not where thy road may lie,
    Or which way mine will be;
If mine will lead thro' parching sands
    And thine aside the sea;
Yet God keeps watch 'tween thee and me,
    So never fear;
He holds thy hand, He claspeth mine,
    And keeps us near.

Should wealth and fame perchance be thine,
    And my lot lowly be,
Or you be sad and sorrowful,
    And glory be for me,
Yet God keep watch 'tween thee and me;
    Both be in His care;
One arm round thee and one round me
    Will keep us near.

I sigh sometimes to see thy face,
    But since this may not be,
I'll leave thee to the care of Him
    Who cares for thee and me.
"I'll keep you both beneath my wings,"
    This comforts, dear;
One wing o'er thee and one o'er me,
    Will keep us near.

And though our paths be separate,
    And thy way is not mine,
Yet coming to the mercy seat,
    My soul will meet with thine.
And "God keep watch 'tween thee and me,"
    I whisper there.
He blesseth thee, He blesseth me,
    And we are near.(1)

Saying goodbye is part of this dynamic life here on earth. It is painful but it is necessary. It is good.

*Lord, thank you for the faith that helps us see the wisdom of your plan. Thank you for love which we share with others near and far. Thank you for the hurt which comes with goodbyes. That hurt lets us know part of us is going with the one from whom we are parting. Thank you for the fall garden which reminds us that there is a time for everything. Thank you for the cycles of life. Amen.*

# The Pompous Grass

*A man's pride will bring him low,*
*But the humble in spirit will retain honor.*
(Proverbs 29:23)

*I*t is fall and I am magnificent. I wish you could see me. I'm part of a huge plant, the tallest vegetation in the entire garden...well, except for the trees of course. I'm strong. The wind blows but does not break me. I'm meant for this spot. This is where I was planted. Here is where I have grown. Nothing will move me. I love it here. I am among others who are just like me.

I've done so well, I'm probably the tallest stalk. I stick up high where I can see all the garden. My seed heads are heavy with ripeness. They bend over in the wind and wave back and forth, but my solid stalk supports them easily. I hold them proudly.

I am ravishing. My leaves are green with golden stripes. That's why I'm called zebra grass. When the sun hits me, as it does in the late afternoon, I glow. My seed heads turn to gold and the light shines through the leaf stripes, turning them amber. Everyone who walks by the garden notices me. They can't help it, I am so elegant.

## The Trimming

What is she carrying? Are those trimmers? What is she going to do? She is walking toward me. No. No. It can't be.  She wouldn't trim me.  I don't need trimming!  The garden books all say to leave me be; to let me stand strong in the winter garden.  Here she comes.  She looks directly at me.  She has Jerry help because I am too big for her.  They cut a few stalks around me.  They cut low and quick.  Maybe she'll not notice me. But I am the tallest and most elegant one.  She is cutting ALL of the tall ones.  She is cutting me!  I am doomed!

Where is she taking me?  What will she do with me?  What's going on here?  NO. NO.  I don't want to go!

### The Urn

It is a mottled blue, about thirty inches tall.  It has a small neck which flows in graceful lines.  It looks symmetrical, Grecian.  It is sitting on the front porch.  It doesn't belong there.  It is much too fine.  Why does she have it there?  Does it have anything to do with me?

### The Living Room

So, here I am along with two dozen others, placed in the blue vase.  We are standing in the corner of the living room.  Actually I fit very nicely  into the decorating scheme.  I have dried.  My seed pods are no longer heavy and hanging.  They have exploded into miniature fireworks.  My leaves have curled.  Some have turned tawny and others have stayed green and striped. I'm still splendid.  It is warm in here.  There is no wind to bounce me around.  No snow or ice will weight me down.  It is very comfortable here.

She gazes at me often.  I can tell she finds me beautiful.  Here I am in an exquisite container.  I am warm, cared for, treasured.  Why was I so worried?  I should have trusted.

*Forgive our arrogance, Lord. Soften us. Touch us. Help us be willing to be moved. Help us know you have plans that we cannot even imagine. Help us trust. Amen.*

# An Autumn Bouquet

*And God said, "See, I have given you every herb that yields seed which is on the face of all the earth, and every tree whose fruit yields seed; to you it shall be for food. Also, to every beast of the earth, to every bird of the air, and to everything that creeps on the earth, in which there is life, I have given every green herb for food"; and it was so. Than God saw everything that He had made, and indeed it was very good. So the evening and the morning were the sixth day.* (Genesis 1:29-31)

*A*ll during the year a bouquet sits on the hallway chest to greet our guests. From spring through the last days of autumn only fresh flowers grace that space. Christmas demands a festive arrangement and during the rest of the winter, dried flowers do the welcoming.

In the fall, a great variety of blooms are available for bouquets. They come in many shapes, textures, and colors. Yellow, burgundy, white, pink, and purple are readily available in our garden.

I love the process of arranging flowers. I take my time and cherish each step. The flowers are cut early in the morning when they are vigorous. The dew is still on the petals and the birds serenade. The blossoms are placed immediately in water. Variety in the blooms; their colors, sizes, and shapes makes an exuberant statement. They call for containers, large enough to support their long stems. The color and shape of the vase must compliment the flowers.

The chosen vase is filled with water. A little bleach and sugar are added to keep the water fresh and to nourish the newly cut blossoms. The flowers are prepared. Extra leaves are removed and the stems are cut on the diagonal so they can draw up water. Each blossom is examined and chosen for its color or shape to fit a certain place in the arrangement. The container is turned around and around as the process continues. Sometimes, another trip outside is needed to find the right flower or greenery for a certain place in the bouquet.

There are some principles of design I follow but each arrangement is unique, depending on what flowers are available. I feel like a partner with God in the creation of beauty. It is a heady, responsible, and gratifying emotion.

Recognizing that I play a role in God's creation is daunting. I am important in the grand scheme of things. Like the individual blossom in the bouquet, I am needed for the very spot where I am. God can use me there.

The creation of a bouquet is on-going. Flowers are short-lived and need to be replaced. My bouquets are not made of plastic or silk. They need tending and caring. The water is changed often.

God's creation is also ever changing. In the grand scheme of things, our individual lives are very short. God uses us where we are to contribute to his creation. The way we care for each other and the environment around us affects the way the universe continues. What a responsibility. What a privilege!

The next time you look at a bouquet, consider the variety that it represents. Contemplate its temporary nature. Reflect on God's creation, the universe, and your part in it. Be humble. Be thankful.

*Creator God,  Thank You for putting us in Your universe.  Help us be alert to Your activity in our lives.  Show the changes You desire us to make, the actions You yearn for us to take, the beauty You provide for us to appreciate.  We are on this earth to take part...to make Your whole creation a more complete bouquet. Enable each of us to understand, accept, and act, following your guidance.  We are deeply gratified to be part of Your creation. Amen.*

*Gardening is a habit of which I hope never to be cured, one shared with an array of fascinating people who helped me grow and bloom among my flowers.*
(Martha Smith)

# Jack's Still There

Jack's still there.
> What do you think of that?

He's shrunk.
> He's no longer tall,
>> barely half his summer size, is all.

His leaves are dry and drooping
> but he is still there.

Sitting on the top of his pulpit
> is a bright red cap.
> It's a seed head...
>> full of potential,
>> full of promise.
>> full of plenty.

Jack's still there.
> What do you think of that?

*The love of gardening
is a seed that once
sown never dies.*
(Gertrude Jekyll)

# Winter

*The* greatest gift of
a garden is the restoration
of the five senses.
(Hanna Rion)

# Ecclesiastes 3:1-8

To everything there is a season,
  A time for every purpose under heaven:
  A time to be born,
    And a time to die;
  A time to plant,
    And a time to pluck what is planted;
  A time to kill,
    And a time to heal;
  A time to break down,
    And a time to build up;
  A time to weep,
    And a time to laugh;
  A time to mourn,
    And a time to dance;
  A time to cast away stones,
    And a time to gather stones;
  A time to embrace,
    And a time to refrain from embracing;
  A time to gain,
    And a time to lose;
  A time to keep,
    And a time to throw away;
  A time to tear,
    And a time to sew;
  A time to keep silence,
    And a time to speak;
  A time to love,
    And a time to hate;
  A time of war,
  And a time of peace.

# Security Blanket

*He sends out His command to the earth;*
*His word runs very swiftly.*
*He gives snow like wool;*
*He scatters the frost like ashes;*
*He casts out His hail like morsels:*
*Who can stand before His cold?*
(Psalm 147:15-17)

*T*he brown plaid wool blanket was always on my bed, and I wanted it there even in the heat of summer. I loved its scent. The binding felt so satiny except when it had been washed. The frayed edge was comforting as I rubbed it under my nose and sucked my thumb. It smelled safe. It was satisfying. I was secure with that blanket wrapped around me.

I wonder if plants feel a sense of protection under a blanket of snow. Snow covers our garden right now. It started to accumulate a couple of weeks ago and is now six to eight inches thick. Each day over the past week an extra half inch has been added, making all pristine. The garden is silent except for the birds.

Snow covers everything with an insulating layer, offering warmth and security. Just before the snow fell I saw many spring bulbs already pushing up through the soil. The warm autumn had fooled them, and I worried about what might happen to them in the dead of winter. Now the deep snow is a blanket that keeps them safe by blocking out the frigid temperatures and thwarting the icy wind. When the snow melts, it will release water for roots and bulbs below and everything will receive an unconditional watering.

These comforters of security remind me of God's unconditional love for everyone. That love blankets us all and is released constantly. God's love is more dependable than snow because it is always there. It never goes away. All we have to do is soak it up and acknowledge its presence.

Oh, how I wish human love was more like God's love --never conditional, deep and available for all, non-judgmental, full of compassion, no strings attached, never withheld, always present.

*Great Lover of us all, help us pattern our love after Yours. May we learn to have compassion for all. Push us to understand the pain of others and reach out to them in constant love. May we be non-judgmental. As Your love blankets us in security, help us share that love with all around us. We know as we share Your love, it is multiplied over all the world. Amen.*

# Winter Worries

*Therefore do not worry about tomorrow,*
*For tomorrow will worry about its own things.*
*Sufficient for the day is its own trouble.*
(Matthew 6:34)

*It's too cold... too soon. The plants won't be hardened. They will freeze.*

*There's not enough mulch. The perennials will be forced out of the soil as the ground freezes, melts, and freezes again.*

*There's too much mulch. The shoots will take too long to come up in the spring.*

*It's been cold for too long. There is not enough snow cover to protect the plants in the bitter cold.*

*There's too much snow. It is weighing down the long limbs on the evergreens.*

*It's too warm too soon. The buds will come out on the flowering trees then they will freeze when we have a cold snap.*

*It's too cold too late....*

What else can I worry about this winter? What about the birds? Do they have enough to eat? What about the rose canes? Jerry didn't prune them back as far as I would have. What about the huge piles of snow, ice, salt, which were thrown on the grass when the road was plowed?

Does worrying help? Can I do anything about the weather? Perhaps, I should move south. I could give up gardening. Non-gardeners don't worry about such things.

I wonder if worrying is our way of hanging on to control. When my children were teenagers, I spent much time concerned about them. They were facing temptations I wasn't sure they could handle. We talked about options. I shared my opinions. We had our family rules, but in the end I knew they had to make the decisions. I could protect them no longer. Their lives were theirs to live. I had to give up control. That was scary and I worried.

Anxiety is a key part of stress. In recent years much has been written about stress and its role in health. Ellen Michaud referred to a disease called generalized anxiety disorder, (GAD) that when ignored can lead to many health problems. (1) Michaud quotes psychiatrist Edward M. Hallowell, MD, an instructor at Harvard Medical School, "Eventually,...every system in the body is affected. You get lower back pain; chest pain; shortness of breath; loss of sexual function; a less vigilant immune system, which leaves you open to cancer; and an increased risk of heart attack and stroke." (2) Included in an extensive list of ways to deal with GAD is prayer or meditation. "Studies show that both meditation and prayer will rebalance your brain chemistry and halt the worry wheel in its tracks." (3)

Scriptural and scientific knowledge are beginning to support each other in areas of physical and mental health. Matthew 6:34 says, "Give your entire attention to what God is doing right now, and don't get worked up about what may or may not happen tomorrow. God will help you deal with whatever hard things come up when the time comes." (The Message, p. 24))

Worry is a waste. It diminishes the beauty of the day. If I can do something to help a situation, then I should do it. Stewing about matters out of my control squanders my time. It can consume me. My energy could be used in more productive and enjoyable ways.

*We know You are in control, Lord. When we acknowledge this truth, we need not worry. Keep us open to your words of comfort. Remind us to bring our concerns to you. Alert us to what we can change and what we cannot. Don't let us waste Your gift of a day by fretting it away. Amen*

# *Through the Window*

*Beloved, let us love one another, for love is of God; and everyone who loves is born of God and knows God. He who does not love does not know God, for God is love.* (1 John 4:7-8 )

The temperature is in the upper twenties and snow has been falling for about three hours. It is hiding the dirty snow mounds left from last week. The driveway and sidewalks are covered. The flakes are small but they fill the air. There is no wind, no drifts. The trees droop. The clumps of tall, golden grass are snow capped and weighted down. The sky is so full of flakes a silvery hue covers all as the snow falls gently.

I sit at the table and look outside. I'm warm, dry, and content. I love looking at the beauty. It touches me and fills me with serenity. My eyes tell my body to get up. Go outside. Fully experience the magic of the moment. My body hesitates. What will I encounter there? How long will I be able to take the cold dampness? What will I see that I can't see from my window seat? Why should I leave this comfort and go out? It will take effort to put on boots, coat, hat, and scarf. My peace will be disturbed. Do I really want to go?

I go.

Outside I experience the snow. I feel it on my nose and cheeks. It tickles as it lands. I am still awed by its beauty. I hear the drip...drip....drip of the icicles. The flakes pause on my coat and I can see their individual splendor. The branches of the red stemmed dogwood stand out in contrast to white. The green holly is iced with crystals. I notice the vapor of my breath. I am worshiping. I am no longer an observer. Standing in the winter garden, I become a participant in God's loveliness.

A fat robin shivers in the tree. There are cat tracks below. I become aware of the birds' peril in this weather. They depend on our feed. In the damp chill, I feel their cold and am aware of their need. In the warmth of the house, I noticed they were at the feeder and was entertained by their eating. Now I become aware of their plight. I am no longer a spectator. I am God's partner in feeding them.

As I walk in the deep snow, I slip and almost fall. There is ice under the fluffy snow. Looking through a window disguised the ice. It was a hidden threat. I hear the sirens in the distance and know someone needs help. The snow is pristine and gorgeous, but treacherous. I am outside for only ten minutes and yet I am much more aware of all around me.

I have to get out into life to know what is truly going on. Seeing life from inside my safe warm home is partial living. I need to take risks. I need to be involved or I will miss much of God's world. If I don't go into the world I won't know how God can use me there.

*Help us be more involved in Your world, God, deeply involved. Give us vision to see the needs. Lift us to respond. Help us live our lives to their fullest. Encourage us to go beyond observing. Push us to get out into life. Empower us to be Your hands and feet, doing Your work. Amen.*

# Holy Hibernation

*So they answered the Angel of the Lord, who stood among the myrtle trees, and said, "We have walked to and fro throughout the earth, and behold, all the earth is resting quietly."* (Zechariah 1:11)

*And He said to them, "The Sabbath was made for man, and not man for the Sabbath."* (Mark 2:27)

Our garden is quiet during the winter months. I see no growth, hear no bees, and smell no sweet fragrances. The ground is covered with snow some of the time or frigid with frost. Everything is hushed and resting. Many plants crave this respite. The cold weather hardens them and destroys pests. Gardeners need the break, a sabbatical, too. They use this time to dream and plan for future beauty. Winter provides plants and people a time for hibernation, a time to restore their energy.

By keeping the Sabbath, humans also can renew themselves on a weekly basis. My religious tradition advises me to keep the Sabbath holy. It says the Sabbath was made for people. That day is a gift. I can use the time to focus, relax, and energize myself. However, my culture tells me it is just another day. If I follow the dictates of society, there is much to do: shopping, eating out, working for double pay, working a second job, catching up on household chores. Which do I believe? Which do I practice?

I want focus in my life and I require time to find, nourish, and keep it. Meditating daily, worshiping regularly, and retreating each season is beneficial. These gifts of time enable me to unite with my maker. These intervals facilitate health. They let me connect with other persons, ideas, and rich beauty. They allow me to consider thoughts and experience feelings that I miss when I fail to pause.

Winter cues many plants and animals to hibernate. Through rest they become stronger. Humans also need holy hibernation.

*Thank you, God, for winter. It is a season for quiet. We can take time to look for the subtle beauty in Your world. We can meditate and visualize how we fit into Your plan and how we can draw closer to You. Thank you for Sabbaths and other opportunities for hibernation. Help us take advantage of these gifts You have given us, and use them for Your glory. Amen.*

*The* person who has planted
a garden feels that he
has done something for
the good of the world.
(Charles Dudley Warner)

# Privileged Pots

*But now, O Lord,*
*You are our Father;*
*We are the clay, and You our potter:*
*And all we are the work of Your hand.*
(Isaiah 64:8)

The garage is filled with pots during the winter. They are stacked together, sitting in corners, on boxes, inside each other. They are waiting to be used. Some are huge, a few are small. Some are decorative, many are utilitarian. Some are cracked, most are dirty. During the growing season they serve a multitude of purposes and are located all over the place. They are on the front porch, patio, in the house, and even in the ground to contain the roots of eager spreaders, like peppermint. We have a use for each pot and we want them where we can find them. In the winter, they are piled in the garage. Gardening would be more difficult with only one type of pot and not nearly as much fun.

Pots move me to think of humanity. Each of us has been created by the Almighty. We are the clay and God is the potter. We are made in all varieties, Christian, Muslim, Hindu, Jew, even non-believers. We come in many colors, nationalities, shapes and sizes. We are fashioned by our creator and each of us has a unique purpose for being. We are privileged pots.

Our world is more interesting because of our differences. The variety adds richness to our lives which I cherish. God wants and needs us all.

We have different tasks for each season in our lives. The challenge is to keep aligned with our "Potter" and find what mission we have been given. Winter is a great season for reflecting about this. Often, during the cold, dark, days we find time for noticing the clues from our maker.

What does God require from you right now? Are you in the middle of parenting some of God's children? Is your career a vehicle for making the world a more loving, safe place? Is God calling you to make use of your talents in a different way? Do you need to learn new skills? Winter is a time for cleaning up, sorting out, and taking steps toward new directions.

I must clean my garden pots and get them ready for the work of spring and summer. I want my creator to cleanse me, also, and prepare me for my tasks in the world.

In the challenges of daily living it is easy to forget that the Potter is really in charge. Winter weather can remind us. When we are snowed in, we know we are not in control. When a loved one dies or a new baby is born, we recognize who is in charge of the universe. We need to be tuned in to the gentle clues around us. When we listen and let God lead, our lives can be part of God's continuing creation.

Even though I may be a clay pot, I know I have a unique place in God's garden. I am--we are cherished vessels.


*Dear Potter, we know You are in charge, but so often we want to do it our own way. Help us remain workable and pliable. Mold us and shape us as You wish. Then use us all through our lives, in each place You put us. Use us for Your purposes. Help us always be aware that You are the potter, we are the clay. Amen.*

# Whose Berries Are They?

*To God our Savior,*
*Who alone is wise,*
*Be glory and majesty,*
*Dominion and power,*
*Both now and forever.*
*Amen.*
                    (Jude 25)

*W*hen we moved into our present home, we decided to take up gardening in a major way. The first project was to redo the landscape in front of the house. We planted some small inexpensive holly bushes, a Blue Prince and three Blue Princesses. We put the females in front of the low living room windows and a male around the corner to provide necessary fertilization. We were promised red berries. We planted in May and waited for the berries to form. Only a few showed up. The plants were too immature. The next spring we discovered that the male plant had died so no berries formed on our holly. We bought a new prince and waited. Gardening is a lesson in patience.

The holly's third growing season got off to a good start. The prince was healthy and so were the three princesses. That spring they were covered with little white blossoms. The holly grew to the window sills. We watched all summer. Green berries turned a vivid red. We were so proud.  They looked exactly as we had envisioned. They kept growing but we put off trimming.  The berry-covered branches were going to enhance our Christmas decorations.  They would look lovely mixed with other evergreens on our mantle.  We needed to wait to prune them.

Wait we did.  September passed and the branches grew. They covered the lower part of the windows.  The bright red berries were in striking contrast to the deep green leaves.  October came.  The berries looked brilliant with the changing of fall colors around the yard.  The bushes were shaggy and badly needed pruning, but we were still waiting for the holidays.  November went and with it most of the color in the yard.  The berries were outstanding.  I could hardly wait to cut those branches.  I visualized putting them in vases in the bedrooms and bathrooms.  I would add them to the table decorations.  They would brighten up everything.  What a luxury to have holly of our very own!

Mid December came.  We bought a tree.  We found extra boughs for the mantle.  Our children and grandchildren were coming for Christmas and we planned to decorate lavishly.  I looked forward to adding fresh holly to the evergreen.  The house would smell wonderful and the holly sprigs would add the final bit of color.  It would be just the right touch.  The next day we planned to cut the holly.

Late in the afternoon I was relaxing in the living room and noticed the holly bushes were full of birds.  I watched, panic stricken, as a flock of robins devoured all of the berries in less than twenty minutes.  No berries were left for decorating.  I couldn't believe it. Those dirty birds had cleaned out the whole crop!  The berries had been my pride and joy.  I had waited for them over three years.  It wasn't fair!  Who had taken care of those bushes?  Who had waited so patiently?  Whose berries were they anyway?

Yes, whose berries are they?

What is God's plan for berries on bushes?  Aren't they to feed the birds?  Aren't they to provide seeds for new hollies? If they also give me enjoyment, then I should be thankful. I had relished the entire process of growing those bushes. God had given me much. God had also taught me a lesson in partnership.

*Almighty Creator, help us remember You have dominion over all the earth. May we be thankful. May we care for Your creation. May we use it with carefulness and gratitude. May we be willing to share with other creatures around us. Amen*

# The Bare Tree

*Blessed is the man who trusts in the Lord,*
*And whose hope is the Lord.*
*For he shall be like a tree planted by the waters,*
*Which spreads out its roots by the river,*
*And will not fear when heat comes;*
*But its leaves will be green,*
*And will not be anxious in the year of drought,*
*Nor will cease from yielding fruit.*
       (Jeremiah 17:7,8)

*I*used to look at winter trees as cold, lonely, and ugly.
I missed the spring and summer green. One cold winter day
I noticed a bare tree silhouetted against a red evening sky. It
resembled lace. Another day, I saw the sun glistening off
the barren branches of a white sycamore. I realized I had
been invited to look closer and to witness God's beauty in
the winter.

In the distance I saw a gnarled old tree. I could see it
was strong. It had grown along the bank of a river where it
had been well watered and nourished. Even though it had
no leaves, I knew it was living. The tree stood completely
bare in the sunlight. The branches soared and reflected the
sun's rays. It had been thriving there for decades.

Since no leaves were on the branches, I could get an
intimate look. Its massive size dwarfed me. I appreciated
the configuration of its limbs. Nests were cradled in its

branches and the gnarled holes surely held secrets. The tree's shortcomings were easy to observe. Some branches were broken. A long scar revealed it had been struck by lightning. Flaws hidden by summer leaves were visible in the winter sun.

I stood in awe looking at this old giant. It was a testament of God's creation. It told of strength, stamina, trouble, refuge. It revealed intricacy, dependance, recovery, and beauty. It detailed life. With a closer look, I saw buds forming at the end of the small branches. They were waiting for the right time to burst forth in blossom. They anticipated precise signals.

What did I learn from the bare winter tree? If I drop some of my defenses, what will others see? How am I sturdy and strong? Where do I offer refuge? Can others see God's beauty in me in spite of flaws? Do others see potential growth? Can they tell I gain my strength from the Lord? Can they tell my roots are grounded in the God of creation who daily nurtures me?

I also noticed in the exposed tree, the contrast of the sturdy trunk, strong limbs, and the tiny lacy tips of the branches. The tree needed all its parts to be vital. The solid structure was needed to support new growth each year. The lacy tips of its branches provided the vulnerable spots where new growth began. We need strength and vulnerability to grow also, and God provides us with both.

*We know You are our creator, God. We want to be like the bountiful trees of summer, full of leaves and fruit. We want to hide our vulnerable parts from others because they show our flaws. Help us know these are our growing points. Support us in sharing these with others. Show us that like the bare tree of winter, Your beauty is within us and will be there for others, if we will let it be seen. Amen.*

# The Forecast Calls for Snow

*To everything there is a season,*
*A time for every purpose under heaven:*
*A time to be born, and a time to die;*
*A time to plant, and a time to pluck what is planted;*
      (Ecclesiastes 3:1-2 )


The garden is just waking up. New green shoots peak through the dirt. I remember the blossoms from last year. They were beautiful, color was rampant. The smell, oh the smell! I can hardly wait for this year's blooms...but wait I must. It is only February and the forecast calls for snow.

    I must wait, I must water, I must weed.
    And while I wait, water, and weed, I will watch.
    I will see. I will touch. I will smell.
    The garden will grow, and I will be part of it.
    But for now, the forecast calls for snow.

    The little green shoots will spread. I will notice the light color turning darker. I will see the contrast of the light green with the darkness of the dirt. I will feel the coolness of the soil in the early morning as I work around the plants. I will notice it's warmth as the day progresses. That soil will be dirt under my nails and I will have to work to get it out. I will watch the plant grow. I will look each day and eventually... I will see little sprouts.  But for now, the forecast calls for snow!

Isn't life like that?  We want tomorrow right now!  As a child we want to be a teenager.  As a teenager - an adult.  The working adult often envies the active retiree who has time to pursue new interests.  In the rush of living we miss the beauty of growing.

But wait...there is beauty in the process.
Take time to notice.
Take time to water, to weed, to grow.
Take time to enjoy tomorrow's snow.

It is February.  It's starting to snow.  It's beautiful!


*Provider God, be with us in our growing. Help us be aware of the beauty in this process. Grant us understanding.  Give us a sense of Your ever present participation in our lives and let us be thankful. May we be aware  that Your plan is good.  Help us trust that plan and have patience. Amen.*

# Jack's There

$\mathcal{J}$ack's there.
>Where?
>>Right there under the frosty leaves.

>I can't see him
>>But I know.
>All of nature tells me
>>Jack's there!

God's here.
>Where?

>>RIGHT HERE!


*Help us be open to You, God, in the changes of the seasons...in everyday occurrences...in our gardens...in our hurting...in our joys. Help us know. You are right here. Amen.*

# References

Garden quotes on pages 21, 32, 35, 41, 64, 66, 73, 79, 95, 98, 100, and 113, are from <u>Garden Gatherings 101 Thoughts from the Garden</u>, edited by Rhonda Hogan.

## Spring

1. <u>The United Methodist Hymnal</u> (The United Methodist Publishing House, Abingdon Press; 201 8th Avenue, South; Nashville, Tennessee 37202, 1989), 314.

2. Kenneth W. Osbeck, <u>One Hundred and One Hymn Stories</u> (Kregel Publications, Grand Rapids, Michigan 49501, 1982), 124-125.

3. Joyce Wilhelmina Sackett, <u>In God's Garden</u> (Tyndale House Publishers, Inc., Wheaton, Illinois 60189), 15.

4. Albert F. Harper, ed., <u>The Wesley Bible, New King James Bible</u> (Thomas Nelson Publishers, Nashville, Tennessee, 1990), 785.

## Summer

1. Albert F. Harper, ed., <u>The Wesley Bible, New King James Bible</u> (Thomas Nelson Publishers, Nashville, TN, 1990), 1788.

2. Eleanor Perenyi, <u>Green Thoughts</u> (Vintage Books Edition, Random House, Inc., 201 E. 50th St., New York, NY 10022, 1983), 254.

3. Marc McCutcheon, <u>Roget's Super Thesauras, Second Edition</u> (Writer's Digest Books, F & W Puplications, Inc., 1507 Dana Ave. Cincinnati, OH 45207), 648.

4. Ola Mae Word, <u>Reflections of Rosedown</u> (Rosedown Plantation and Gardens, St. Francisville, LA 70775), 33-34.

5. Ibid., 46.

*Autumn*

    1. Hazel Felleman, ed., <u>The Best Loved Poems of American People</u>, (Doubleday and Company, Inc., Garden City, NY, 1936), 304.

*Winter*

    1. Ellen Michaud, "When Worrying Becomes Deadly," <u>Prevention</u>, (Rodale, 33 E. Minor St., Emmaus, PA 18098., Feb. 2000, Vol. 52, Issue 2.), 136.
        2. Ibid., 137.
        3. Ibid., 139.

# To order this book...

Please send check and order to:
    LTL Publishing
    1545 Austin Drive
    Columbus, OH 43220
    (614) 451-3789

Copies of this book may be purchased for $13.95 per copy plus $0.80 sales tax (for Ohio residents) and a $2.00 charge per book for handling and shipping.

On your order indicate:
    Number of books
    Name
    Shipping address
    Telephone number and/or e-mail address

## The author...

Marjorie Sharples is a retired elementary school counselor, mother of three and grandmother of eight. Since retiring she has become an avid gardener. This new hobby has given her opportunity to notice and appreciate nature in a garden setting. Though she has written professionally as a counselor, this is her first book of devotions. She is an active member of Bethel United Methodist Church in Columbus, Ohio.

## The photographer...

Tennyson Williams is retired from his careers as family physician and professor of Family Medicine at The Ohio State University. Photography has always been a serious pastime. Now it is a passion. His creative photos grace the covers of professional journals and enhance many exhibits. He also is a member of Bethel United Methodist Church.